j968.064 Cooper, Floyd.
MANDELA
      Mandela.

$15.95

DATE			

Dedicated to the memory and spirit of
Arthur Ashe

MANDELA

from the life of the
South African statesman

FLOYD COOPER

PHILOMEL BOOKS

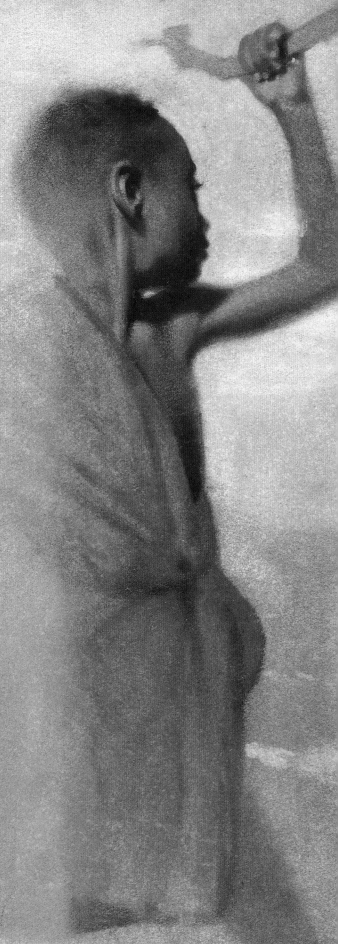

He was born on July 18, 1918 at Mvezo, a tiny village on the banks of the Mbashe River in South Africa. His name, Rolihlahla, was the Xhosa way of saying "pulling the branch of a tree," or "troublemaker." But his family called him Buti.

Always, the wind had blown mightily through the valley that cradled his village. Sunsets had forever before kissed the hills, where little boys played and romped and did their chores. Life there was as it always had been.

Buti's ancestors were rulers of the proud Thembu people who had lived in this rich land for generations. His own father, Gadla Hendry Mphakanyiswa of the Mandela family, was chief of the village, a proud chief who ruled with a stubborn sense of fairness and tradition. He was a counselor to kings, as were his father and his grandfather before him.

When it was time, Buti would be told these things about his country and about the wind that blew through the valley that cradled his village. And he too would lead.

Chief Hendry knew this and was happy.

Then one day, when Buti was still a baby, an ox belonging to one of Chief Hendry's subjects wandered into a neighbor's *kraal*. The neighbor, thinking only about his good fortune, ate the ox. When the chief ordered the man to pay for eating the ox, the neighbor complained to the English magistrate. The magistrate ordered Chief Hendry to appear before him, but he stubbornly refused. A Thembu chief had only to answer to the Thembu king, not any English magistrate.

Because of his refusal, Chief Hendry was dethroned. Standing firm for what he believed cost Buti's father his cattle, his wealth, and his chieftainship. The Mandela family, now poor, had to move to a new village.

The new village, Qunu, was not very different from Mvezo. The wind blew through the valley, and the sunsets had forever kissed the hills. Buti's mother tended the fields of vegetables. His sisters ground the mealies and prepared the pumpkin, beans, and sorghum for dinner. Buti herded the cattle. Although Buti's father was no longer chief, he was respected, and would often be called to settle a dispute or instruct a student in history. And he would storytell about the days of forever before.

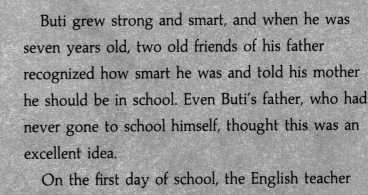

Buti grew strong and smart, and when he was seven years old, two old friends of his father recognized how smart he was and told his mother he should be in school. Even Buti's father, who had never gone to school himself, thought this was an excellent idea.

On the first day of school, the English teacher gave all the African children English names. Buti's new name was Nelson.

He wasn't certain if he liked his new English name, but Nelson knew he liked school. He liked the slate tablets used for writing. He liked learning new things and he liked the way his father prepared him for school by telling him always to stand firm for what he believed was fair and right.

One day, when Nelson was nine years old, his father came home early, very ill. He called Nelson, and they talked the words of school-day mornings. He told Nelson always, always to stand firm for what he believed was fair and right. Soon after, his father died.

The wind in the valley that cradled the village blew on, as it always had. But Nelson had gone as far as he could in the school at Qunu. It was time to leave his beloved mother, sisters, and his beloved village for a new school. For this, he must journey to the capital of Thembuland, a neighboring village called Mqhekezweni.

It was a long walk to Mqhekezweni. Nelson and his mother, who took him to the new place, walked on hard, thorny roads, past many villages without stopping. Finally they arrived. The village was like no village Nelson had ever seen before! He saw lush gardens, apple orchards, and maize fields surrounded by peach trees. He saw two rectangular houses, seven round houses ("rondavels," they were called), and a large, honking motorcar. Never would he fit into such a grand place as this!

Nelson was shy and lonely when his mother said good-bye, but as she disappeared over the hill, she knew that the things that awaited Nelson here would prepare him for a bigger, wider world.

Helping Nelson to overcome his shyness was his new family, the family of Chief Jongintaba Dalindyebo. The chief, a distant relative of Nelson's, owed a debt to Nelson's father. Wasn't it Nelson's father who had used his influence to make Jongintaba a chief! And so, Chief Jongintaba and his wife, No-England, took Nelson into their family and raised him as if he were their own.

Nelson shared a rondavel with Justice, the chief's son, who was four years older than Nelson. Together with Justice's sister, Nomafu, they played hard, they studied hard, and they went to Sunday school. The three grew strong and smart.

Nelson thought Mqhekezweni a magnificent place. It was called the Great Place. There, important visitors from all over Thembuland gathered to hold court, to debate, to chat and tell stories. How Nelson listened. And he learned many things at the foot of the chieftains and elders. One very old storyteller was Zwelibhangile Joyi. Old Chief Joyi, with his wrinkled blue-black skin and dry, dusty voice, had lived and seen much from the days of forever before. He entranced the gathered elders, telling ancient tales of great kingdoms like the Zulu and Xhosa, of brave warriors like Ngangelizwe, who fought the British, and of wise kings like Ngubengcuka, who united the Thembu people.

Nelson was most entranced of all. The image of Old Chief Joyi, nimbly stepping like an attacking warrior as the smoky firelight flickered across his moist brow, telling a history not to be found in any book, would remain with Nelson always.

Like a large mimosa tree, Nelson grew sturdy and tall. When he was sixteen, it was time for him to become a man. He journeyed to Tyharlarha, on the banks of the Mbashe River. With the tribal elders guiding them, he and other young men his age rubbed their bodies from head to toe with white clay and put on the traditional grass skirts. They danced. The elders told fables and tales, and finally performed the rites of manhood. Nelson Mandela was now a man.

Nelson had even more responsibilities after this. Not only did he tend the herds and milk the cows, he ran errands for Chief Jongintaba and looked after other matters of business for him. Important work for a young man!

Even so, school stood foremost in Nelson's life. In order to be a counselor to kings, like his father before him, and his grandfather before him, and on forever before, Nelson had to learn more about what Chief Jongintaba called the "wide world." He needed more education. Chief Jongintaba wouldn't have it any other way.

The chief sent both Justice and Nelson to the best African schools in South Africa. Nelson went to Clarkebury Institute, a Thembu college. There Nelson met Thembu people from other villages and cities. And for the first time in his life, he shook hands with a white man, the governor of the college, known as a white Thembu because he loved and understood the Thembu people.

Then Nelson joined Justice at Healdtown, the largest African school below the equator. For the first time, Nelson became friends with people from different tribes—the Sotho, Swazi, and Zulu—and for the first time he saw himself as not just a Thembu or Xhosa, but as an African.

Next Nelson advanced to Fort Hare, a missionary college for African scholars from all over Africa. Here he studied hard, but it wasn't all work! He joined the track team and learned to dance. He became a school leader, too, and in his final year was elected to serve on the student council. When, in a protest for better food, he quit the council, the principal threatened him: come back, or be expelled!

Nelson refused. He stood firm for what he believed was fair and right, and was expelled.

Nelson returned home, but when Chief Jongintaba learned of his stubbornness, he was furious! He ordered Nelson to return to school, and to rejoin the student council. End of discussion.

Nelson would obey, but until the session began, he enjoyed life as it was always before, herding, looking after matters for the chief. Then one evening, the chief summoned Justice and Nelson to a meeting.

He told them he had selected a bride for each of them. Before he journeyed to the land of his ancestors, he wanted to see his two sons properly married. The dowries had been paid. The marriages would take place immediately!

The chief was merely being a chief—arranging marriages for his children. But Justice and Nelson returned to their rondavel with their heads down. Neither liked the bride that had been picked for him. The two young men decided instead to run away.

Choosing a moment when the chief would be away on business, the lads took two of his prized oxen and sold them for a good price. Then using some of the money to buy passage, they climbed on a train going to Johannesburg, the city of gold.

They arrived just as darkness was settling. Jeweled, flickering lights spread out like spilled treasure. Nelson had heard many stories about Johannesburg. Each year thousands of young men made their way to the gold mines there, seeking fame and fortune. What they found instead was a hard life working long hours in underground darkness for little pay and a dry, wheezing cough as a bonus. Sometimes these people never returned home.

Justice and Nelson were spared such a fate. Because of their royal ancestry, Nelson was made a guard and Justice a clerk. Very soon, however, word of their whereabouts reached Chief Jongintaba. He angrily demanded they return, but this time Nelson, with the winds of all that had come before at his back, stood firm.

Nelson persuaded the chief to let him remain in Johannesburg to continue his schooling at the University of South Africa. But where would he live? How would he pay for school? There is an old Xhosa saying: "People are people through other people." And so Nelson found a place to live with a Xhosa family in Alexandra, one of the few places in Johannesburg where blacks were allowed to live.

This district was overcrowded with small matchbox-type houses that had no plumbing, no electricity, and no heat. Most had tin roofs and dirt floors.

Nelson apprenticed at a law firm during the day, earned a small salary, and went to school at night. These were very poor times for Nelson. For five years straight, he wore a suit given to him by his boss at the law firm. He once said that the suit was patched in so many places it was more patches than suit.

Nelson never imagined the unfairness and inequality that he would find in Johannesburg. He'd known of the attitude most Englishmen had toward anything African (hadn't he had to take an English name on his first day of school?). But he could hardly believe what he saw.

If you were black, you could live only in reserved areas. You could leave only to work in the city, and whenever you left, you had to carry a little book called a "pass book." If you were caught without it, you were thrown into prison. You paid a special tax. You rode "African only" buses, drank from "African only" water taps, and were snubbed and insulted daily. What could possibly happen to any person's pride and self-worth under such terrible conditions?

Nelson couldn't bear to see people treated unjustly. They couldn't better their condition—not because they weren't capable, but because opportunity was taken away from them by laws made to "keep them in their place." This was not the way of Chief Joyi's stories about kings who ruled their subjects with an equal hand! This was not the way it was in the days of forever before.

But nothing stopped Nelson from finishing law school. In fact, he and a partner, Oliver Tambo, opened the doors to the first black law practice in Johannesburg.

At the same time, Nelson began to attend meetings and rallies held by other people who didn't like the unfairness and inequality of the South African government. They wanted change! Their numbers grew and grew, and included not only black people—doctors, lawyers, teachers, artists, writers—not only Indians and other people of color, but many white people.

Yet even as they met, new laws were being created. There were separate doors for blacks and whites in restaurants and stores, separate trains, separate schools, separate restrooms! And the schools, neighborhoods, and restrooms for blacks were far inferior to those for whites. This system of government was called "apartheid," or apart. And these gatherings of people who were against apartheid called themselves the African National Congress or ANC.

Nelson became a strong leader of the African National Congress. He wanted Africans to be able to vote! He wanted apartheid to end! Sometimes now he planned strikes and marches and protests.

Sometimes now demonstrators were rounded up by the police, Nelson among them! Sometimes people were killed. Still Nelson's life was filled with his passion to stand firm in the face of the inequities he saw.

Nelson married Evelyn Mase in 1945, and then, following their divorce, he married Winnie Madikizela in 1958—both women who were not chosen for him by anyone else. In time he had two sons and three daughters.

Thembi was his firstborn. Even as Nelson practiced law, and met and marched, he found time to play with his young son, Thembi, sometimes at the very rocky knoll where protests had been held. One might see them there on an evening, playing and romping as the wind whistled through the great stones, just as it had always done forever before.

Thembi began to know of his father and was proud. But by now, other people in Johannesburg, many white people, began to know about Nelson Mandela and his stand against apartheid, and were angry.

One night, in the still darkness, Thembi was awakened by an awful crash! The door to the Mandela home was smashed in, and four men dressed in khaki rushed in and ransacked everything in the house! Three of the men grabbed Nelson Mandela, and in front of his little boy and wife, dragged him through the door! Like the whoosh of a hurricane, the men came and went. The South African police had taken Nelson Mandela to jail.

Nelson Mandela would be arrested many times over the years and eventually let go. But finally, in 1963, in Rivonia, he was charged with attempting to overthrow the state of South Africa. The only question was: would he be put to death, or sent to prison for the rest of his life?

There was no wind in the courtroom when he stood before this judge. No wind at his back, whispering "Stand firm!" The only wind this day was the wind that blew through the black townships of South Africa: Alexandra, Sophiatown, Sharpeville, and Soweto.

The wind moaned for justice! The wind cried for fairness! Even in the face of losing his own life, Nelson Mandela stood firm that day for what he believed was fair and right, but he was sent to prison.

The prison was called Robben Island. Nelson Mandela remained there for twenty-seven years, stubbornly holding firm for what he believed. But even while he was there, his spirit carried all across South Africa, joined by youthful shouts for freedom: Amandla! Amandla Ngawethu! Power to the people!— until the walls of apartness, apartheid, crashed right down.

Released from prison on February 11, 1990, Nelson Mandela helped create a new constitution for South Africa and became the first president of the new government in an election in which all Africans voted.

Son of chiefs, fighter for equality, he had stood firm.

AUTHOR'S NOTE

Nelson Mandela was born on July 18, 1918, in Mvezo, a small country village on the banks of the Mbashe River, in the Transkei region of South Africa. Born into royalty, he learned leadership early from his father, who was chief of Mvezo and a counselor to the kings of Thembuland. Like his father and his grandfather before him, Nelson was groomed to be an advisor to the throne, but he was also taught by his father to stand up for what was just and fair. These teachings would be the base, the very strong foundation that would allow Nelson to endure the insufferable torments he would later face as a man.

And face them he would.

A member of the active African National Congress as early as 1943, he eventually became president of its Youth League, and a spokesman for it. He was labeled a "banned" man by the government and was arrested many times during the next years. Even so, in 1945 he married Evelyn Mase and fathered two sons and a daughter, and in 1953 finally fulfilled his dream of setting up his own legal practice with his friend Oliver Tambo. And in 1958, after divorcing Evelyn Mase, he married activist Winnie Madikizela, with whom he had two more daughters.

It was in 1963 in the infamous Rivonia Trial that Nelson Mandela was charged with sabotage and attempting to overthrow the state. Though he stood to receive the death penalty, he never wavered from what he truly believed. He was found guilty and sentenced to life in prison on Robben Island. Even during this prison ordeal, he continued to champion the cause of equality.

Indeed, with unwavering courage and unyielding strength, Nelson Mandela would maintain his ground: his belief that no man is free unless all men are free and equal. He would hold firm against the raw headwinds of injustice until they became the tailwinds of equality, lifting his country to a higher place.

It was this determination that would lead him, along with South Africa's president F.W. de Klerk, to win the 1993 Nobel Peace Prize for drafting the first democratic South African constitution, in which blacks were made full citizens and had the right to vote. It was this determination that would lead him to be elected South Africa's first black president in May 1994.

And so, Mandiba, it is like a father that we love and admire you, for it is like a father that you teach us to be strong and to stand firm for what we believe is fair and just.

Floyd Cooper

PRONUNCIATION KEY

Amandla Ngawethu	(ah-MAND-la n-gah-WAY-too)
apartheid	(ah-PAR-tide)
Buti	(BOO-tee)
Jongintaba Dalindyebo	(jong-een-TAH-bah dahl-ind-JAY-boh)
kraal	(KRAWL)
Madikizela	(mah-DEE-kee-zay-lah)
Mbashe	(m-BAH-shay)
Mphakanyiswa	(m-pah-kah-NEE-swah)
Mqhekezweni	(m-kay-KAH-zwee-nee)
Mvezo	(m-VAY-zoh)
Ngangelizwe	(n-gahn-geh-LEE-zway)
Ngubengcuka	(n-goo-BEN-choo-kah)
Qunu	(KOO-noo)
Rolihlahla	(RHOH-lee-hlah-hlah)
rondavel	(ron-DAH-vuhl)
Thembi	(TEM-bee)
Thembu	(TEM-boo)
Xhosa	(KHOH-zah)
Zwelibhangile Joyi	(zway-lee-bahn-GEE-lay JOY-ee)

Note: Buti may also be spelled "Bhuti."

BIBLIOGRAPHY

Benson, Mary. *Nelson Mandela: The Man and the Movement*. New York: W. W. Norton & Company, 1994.

Mandela, Nelson. *Long Walk to Freedom: The Autobiography of Nelson Mandela*. Boston: Little, Brown and Company, 1994.

Meer, Fatima. *Higher Than Hope: The Authorized Biography of Nelson Mandela*. New York: Harper & Row, 1990.

Special thanks to Johann and Marjorie van Heerden,
Wanita Kawa, Sandi Majikija of the University of Fort Hare
in South Africa, and the South African consulate in
New York City.

Patricia Gauch, Editor

Library of Congress Cataloging-in-Publication Data
Cooper, Floyd. Mandela: from the life of the
South African statesman / written and illustrated by Floyd Cooper.
p.   cm.   1. Mandela, Nelson, 1918-   —Juvenile literature.
2. Presidents—South Africa—Biography—Juvenile literature.
I. Title.   DT1949.M35C66   1996   968.06'4'092—dc20   [B]
95-19639   CIP   AC   ISBN 0-399-22942-6
10 9 8 7 6 5 4 3 2 1   First Impression